i

Disabled Monsters

Disabled Monsters

by

John C. Mannone

The Linnet's Wings Press

Copyright Notice

Ordering Information:
Single Copies available from our website:
www.thelinnetswings.org
Quantity sales. Special discounts are available on quantity purchases by corporations, associations, and others. For details, mail the publisher at the address above.

ISBN-978-0-9930493-8-5

Editor: Marie Fitzpatrick

Layout and Design: Marie Fitzpatrick

OFFICES

Online: Zoetrope Virtual Studio,

The Linnet's Wings Submission Office

Surface:

Design, Carchuna, Granada, Spain

Publishing, Mullingar, Co. Westmeath, ROI

Other Publications by The Linnet´s Wings

Classic: "The Song of Hiawatha" by Henry Wadsworth Longfellow ISBN 13: 978-1480176423

Classic: "The House that Jack Built" by Randolph Caldecott, ISBN-13: 978-1483977669

"One Day Tells Its Tale to Another" by Nonnie Augustine ISBN-13: 978-1480186354

"About the Weather—Spring Trending" by Marie Lynam Fitzpatrick ISBN-13: 978-0993049330

"This Crazy Urge to Live" by Bobby Steve Baker ISBN-13: 978-0993049-0-9

"A Christmas Canzonet" (Classic and Contemporary Poets, and Classic Art) ISBN-13: 978-1522710714

Acknowledgments

Disabled Monsters is a poetic metaphor on how people cope with physical, mental, emotional and behavioral disability, including disease, depression and death.

I gratefully acknowledge the following venues that first published twenty of these thirty poems in this collection.

The American Headache and Migraine Association ("The Devil's Head Games")
Dads of Disability, Gary M Dietz ("The iPod" [1])
Enchanted Conversation: A Fairy Tale Journal ("Affective Disenchantment" [2])
The Legendary ("Empty Shell," "Orange Peels")
Liquid Imagination ("Genesis of Fear" [3])
Nostrovia! Poetry ("Blue")
Mirror Magazine ("The Doctor's Daughter")
Poetry Pacific ("Diamonds")
She Asks For Slippers While Pointing at the Salt, Inglis House ("Hauntings" [4])
Skive Magazine ("Death Approaches")
Songs of Eretz Poetry Review ("Alternative Medicine")
Tipton Poetry Journal ("Mulberry Leaves")
Vermillion Literary Project ("Cornsilk and Violets")
The Walking Project, The Institute of Disabilities/Temple University ("Stepping Out")
Whistling Skin Anthology, Swimming With Elephants Press ("Light Blooms")
Wordgathering: The Journal of Disability Poetry ("The Dogwood," "Leaving Shadows," "The Gift," "A Sweet Kind of Blindness")

[1] Won first place (judged by Marly Youmans and one of the four poems in the book)·

[2] Won first place in the poetry category of the "Beauty and the Beast" writing contest 2010.

[3] Won third place in the Beginner Writers Contest 2010.

[4] Won first place in the Sixth Annual Inglis House Poetry Contest 2009 and was nominated for the Pushcart Prize in poetry.

Dedication:

For Wanda, whose heart does the seeing for her

Table of Contents

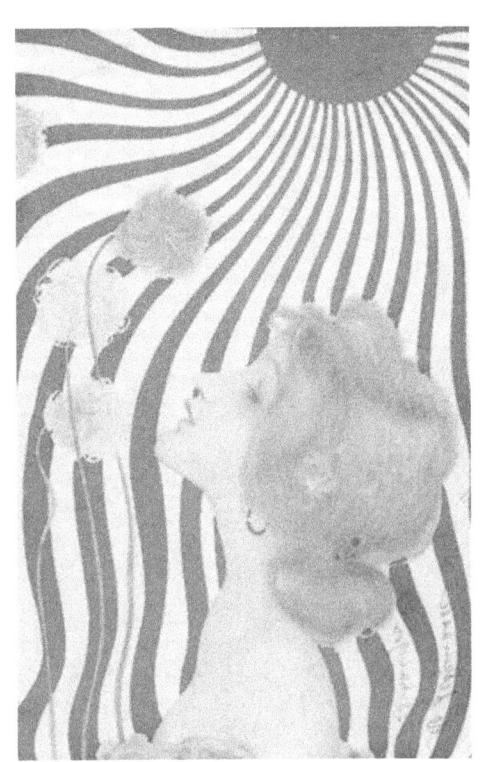

Prologue:

Hope is the thing with feathers
That perches in the soul,
And sings the tune without the words,
And never stops at all
—Emily Dickinson

The wound is the place where the light enters you.
—Rumi

This is love: to fly toward a secret sky, to cause a hundred
veils to fall each moment. First to let go of life. Finally, to
take a step without feet.
—Rumi

Empty Shell

All mankind is of one author,
and is one volume; when one man dies,
one chapter is not torn out of the book,
but translated into a better language.
—John Donne

The ocean waves slap
as if turning one watery
page after another
in a chapter of its life.

There's an echo
on the beach, the swish
of sand, the clink of pebbles,
the clatter of death
from an empty mussel.
Its shell, a palace, a coffin.

An insignificant piece of sand,
irregular glass perhaps,
edges the tender flesh, pokes,
irritates the mantle membrane.
Exacerbated,

shuttles that grain by peristalsis
until worn smooth by magic
of chemistry

and slow lapse of time.
Refreshing of salt.

Strange symbiosis—
blue oyster with green sea
—forming nacreous orb
translucent to a light
that it may never see.
It has no glow of its own.

Why is the pearl hidden
inside the folds of darkness?

The pearl, as if a perfect
period, marks the end
of the sentence in its chapter
given to the waves.

The Dogwood

Do you think there's someplace where we can meet
that's not in silence and not in sound
—Children of a Lesser God (1986)

You can only hear the silence
in the wind. The tree sways
its arms, crossing them, fingers
moving in the weave of its hands,
as if to sign. You can read
the quaking of leaves telling us
the quiet truth—we are not
the children of a lesser God.

Inside my mind, I see your soul
and the color of your words
that you translate for me. I feel
the texture of their meaning
and hear the rocks cry out with us.

This tree, too, reads words to me,
to my fingers running over its trunk,
and Braille branches, over invisible
veins in the leaves; it whispers
in the flowers. I hear it bleed.

Blue

Part 1. In a Maze of Rooms

One was all blue like the ocean:
the ceiling, light as sky; walls darkening
deep blue to the floor. Wallpapered fish
flamed orange on the walls, vibrating
their colors.

I could hear a symphony of hums,
the flutter of fins brushing waves
with paint. As fish shook, scales dropped
drifting slowly to the edge of the wall
sinking to the floor.

There, an iridescence, a growing glitter,
then colors exploded into sea spray
misting room. Drops shimmered as I
sifted each shape and color, every shade
of feeling.

I piled in the corner, all the sad pieces.
The happy ones swirled as I moved
my fingers across the wall, through air,
they all fell into place—a mosaic
painting the heart of the universe.

It was more than a pattern; it throbbed

music, pulsed magic—equations
making sense of this world. I could feel
their color, and their sobbing. The sobbing
behind me growing louder. I knew the voice

of my little sister—stooped in the corner,
her eyes were wet. And mine were also.
We could hear the universe cry within
our single mind. We held each other tight.

Part 2. The Color of Sadness

Do you think Mom can hear us?
I call to her, but she still cries.
I can make my mouth move here
in this room. Justin, what's wrong
with them?
        I don't know, Katie,
I tossed them every note of music
dancing in this room, every shade
of blue I found and kissed each one
before they fluttered from my fingers.

Reality TV

I told the attendant to flick on channel 50/51.
The six o'clock show was about to begin.

The soldier coming home from Iraq,
the newsman said, wasn't an IED victim,
but I could see her cratered eyes, her spirit
blown to smithereens. Fragments

of her memory sifted her wet eyes:
the carnage, bodies rotting in ditches,
the snapping recoils of the M16 silenced
in her head, in my head.

Detach yourself. Don't ask why.
Don't wonder, *What if?*

But how do I divorce
reality of horror from fantasy of peace?

Entropy prohibits my coming together
from chaos, at least not without help.

But what help? *Xanax, Prozac, Thorazine?*
They fool you into thinking truth
is asleep or not pointed, its edges not sharp.
Who can forget death, destruction?
Who can forget hopelessness, helplessness?

I cannot forget… the loneliness.

Hell, I don't understand why
it is so hard to breathe. They say
it's posttraumatic stress, or is it
a convenient scapegoat for my failures?

I am so scared, life is slipping,
yet in death, I would remain shattered,
otherwise, I would welcome it.

His white shoes shuffle across
the checkered tiles back to the console.

I remain a blank screen,
everything is black and white
TV hiss.

Leaving Shadows

Green-brown mottle of khaki clothes
camouflages him sniping in foliage,
late noon Mekong sun sweating
through the long Banyans of Vietnam.

He lies still on limbs without limbs
leaves stripped like chaff,
machine guns strafing shadows.

Choppers find him among pale leaves
tinted red as in eclipse of moon,
then the moon moved leaving shadows
on the limb illumined by the sun.

~~~

Jungle shadows flicker with the vertigo
of recollected sounds, even in New York,
each time he passes under branches
limned in lazy sun. The umbral elms

and maples transform to Mangroves
through the spokes,
the shiny spokes of his chair, reflecting
each memory leaving shadows.

Hauntings

No rain to wash the heat away
its waves buffet our faces
soak into our khakis blending
with the desert drab, pale
structures, empty freedoms.

My platoon, in stealth, combs
the quiet buildings, empty rooms.
Hiding in the corner, a mother, baby
snuggled in her hijab, for a moment,
the Madonna and Child,
my wife and son in Minneapolis-St. Paul.
I hear their whimpers, their prayers.

I step toward them, feel
the click, wood against metal,
as if a poltergeist unlatched the pin.
I fling myself on top the woman,
her death muffled
from deafening grenade, shrapnel
meant for her, carving my ears.

Block and timber straddle us,
my back wedges rafters, legs lever,
arms undergird the beams, heave
outstretched to free the woman
and her child.

I couldn't hear the second click.
The explosion that left my limbs
in Fallujah, hands still gripping
two-by-fours.

That dismembered house, its soul
leaked out, inrushed with nightmares
of urban bombs, the ghost of men.
It can't feel
its family through the rubble,
the concrete, the lumber debris.
They'd rebuild the house,
the haunting remains.

Doctors said I'd be alright,
but no one warned me
of the demons hanging on
ends of nerves. Haunted by ghost
pain, prosthetics for disembodi-
ments with no memory for fingers.

I can no longer hear the beating
of the distant drums, or hearts,
only the static hiss of its snare,
your voice lost in gray noise.

I am haunted by the sound
of your voice. I am haunted
by the touch of your breasts.

The Gift

The black vinyl of an old record caught the eerie sheen of the living room light. Like a lavender wave, light crested the spinning ridges. I heard the pops and hiss as if water spumed on rocks with a rhythm of splashes in sync with the warbled platter dancing on the turntable. It subsumed me. I submerged into music just below the surface. I felt each jazz note wash over me as cool salt surf; my feet working hard against the surge, until I blended with the sea that swept me into my past where I could waltz with you while the minstrels played our song, and Sachmo sang *What a Wonderful World*. This gift. A world of sound so different from Vietnam, where I can hold you close to me, and dance the past away. Where I no longer need these phantom legs.

Disabled Monsters

I

Vagaries of the mind,
     of the body
are *deaf, dumb and blind,*

yet we stalk incessantly
    to ravage you.

Don't we all feel
like the living dead
     because of fears
   and limitations?

II

Full moons might bring
    werewolves,
even the ones deaf

to our own howls, deaf
to your screams.

We feel the ground vibrate,
read the tremors
   of your hearts
with our sharp-clawed toes.

We smell your fear.

Close in. See you
in the dark better than any
Lon Chaney werewolf.

There is no escaping
our slashing
        of your jugulars.

There is no escaping
the ringing, your ears
        deafened by silence.

III

Not all vampires
see eye-to-eye,
some are *blind as bats*.

But do not be deceived,
        we hear
        your blood
coursing through veins,

        that faint sound
        of air in your lungs.

We're driven by lust
        for blood.
We'll hunt you down.

When we catch you,
and we will,
we'll bat you around

as a cat would a mouse.

Our teeth
do not need to see
to cut your throats.

You can pray,
it doesn't matter.
We're blind

to the crucifix
and silver rosary,
to the holy.

Unlike Bram Stoker's
Dracula, our flesh,
immune to sun,
will not disintegrate
            to ash.

IV

We are deaf
and we are blind.
Yet you'll feel the monsters
            press in.

I will not be a victim, you say.
Don't be dumb.

Even zombies
do not stop to die.

14

Go ahead, call the titular *Blade*
    to silver-dagger
    the vampire,

go get St. George
    to long-sword
     the slant-eyed dragon,

don't listen
    to the telltale heart
    beat against time,

or look
    at Medusa
    turn your insides
    to stone,

we are all disabled
    monsters.

Stepping Out

Falling
with each step falling
deliberately when we move off
the stature of stillness balanced by two feet

spread out
we begin to fall and try
to fool the fall by stepping out
catching ourselves before the tumbling of legs

and humbling
by gravity on our attempt
to maintain balance moving forward
in dynamic equilibrium falling and catching

falling
and catching the instability
of the whole thing that is called walking

A Sweet Kind of Blindness

*I would rather have thirty minutes of wonderful
than a lifetime of nothing special.*
—Steel Magnolias, 1989

I never thought of sugar as a poison
of sweet dreams and visions
of family or its bittering of body parts—

arms purpled with tracks
vestiged from some machine
that flushes urine from you,

every nerve charged with electric waves
from surge of chemistry
coaxing tears that blind me, too.

I squeeze your hand; close my eyes so I can see
the same black screen on my retina
and let memories paint images there.

There, your smiles blur with saline drops
reflect as foveal mirrors, fading in and out
as sanguine rings from squint of pressure—

a sweet kind of blindness
that lets you see the magic of a kiss,
not just the feel of it,

waiting for the touch of alchemy
to smooth sweet seconds into hours,
lead into gold.

Pain as sweet as sugar

Pain as sweet as sugar
barstools in on a wing-beat
of a fractured heart. Drunk,

staggers like old love,
now a fossil I can hold
in my hands. Sweet fire

on my lips, a burn
in my throat, delirium
of lake-effect snow

fluttering in my chest.

Affective Disenchantment

Be so kind and bring me a rose
—Beauty and the Beast

When I met you in the dawn,
I forced my intrepid monster
inside to hide. Your smiles
trumped my fears and held
my beast in dark recesses.

You found me
beneath the grotesque,
and my uncomely pride.
Crimson washed the mornings,
shone on your golden tresses,
and I kissed you between
the stone statues in the garden
of roses. We felt sparkles of light.

You became my bride.
But pale blue afternoons
waned the passion
until only night showed naked
stars and empty eyes.

Your mood had changed.
Soothing smiles no longer
there to quell the ogre inside.
I clawed the night.

Today I feel ugliness inside
poking through disheveled hair,
through eyes blackened with wet
glitter of regret. And I walk
in the shadow of your beast.

Beneath the Surface

Let me sink
into the mirror of your eyes
deep into your heart. Let me
pulse with your ocean there,
float with wind-driven crests.
I can taste the salt, slide
with the froth and the foam
cupped by swell of waves.
I am buoyed by dark depths
where memories drown. Let me
hold your hand tightly
while you breathe
for me.

The Doctor's Daughter

He stethoscopes her heart, senses its swish, its race against the ambiguity
of night. Gently probes her chest, back; her flesh trumpeting auscultations
through the plum wood tube touching doctor's ear: the gurgling, the flutter
in her lungs that struggle to soak air. Her small body swelters with heat,
the cotton nightgown drenches with fever. Sleep labors against discomfort
in her throat, red, raw, as if rasped by blackberry briars—muting moans.

His slender fingers grasp the small leather duffel; rummages for hope hiding
in its supple folds. Gropes for something, anything inside the black mouth
of his bag: bandages, metal tools, rubbing alcohol, wintergreen oil, tincture
of iodine, vial with faded brown paper—*Astringent: Extract of Persimmon*
(also useless for healing cuts of heart).

But she dreams of dancing with sugar plum fairies and of other fairy tales,
while he wishes to whisk her far away into strawberry fields in his own.
If only the diagnosis were wrong or plaintive prayers answered right now;
if blurring tears would wash away with whiskey. Instead, he staggers
among the violets, the lilacs, and the thorns next to the poplar tree draping
the limestone rocks etched with his daughter's name…and with her sister's.

~~~

Postscript: Before the invention of streptomycin, the disease called
"consumption" victimized children. Also known as tuberculosis, it was the
biggest killer disease in the 19th century.

The Healing

I swear by all the gods to keep
according to my ability, my judgment,
the following Oath and agreement:

To consider dear to me, as my parents,
him who taught me this art …
                    —Adapted from "The Hippocratic Oath"

The room, sullen by darkness, yields
to dawn's prescription—soft light
brushing her cheeks.

The I.V. bottle catches glints. Intensive
Care. Labyrinth of tubes. Hospital
gown half-hiding the ripples of ribs, scars.

Cardiac monitor beeps incessantly
with threats of fibrillation—unsilenced
haunts of low oxygen level alarms.

Computer screens blink data as the nurse
clacks on the keyboard, pushes buttons
by bedpost instruments. The doctor tries

to betray the numbers with whispers.
But even soft words cut like a knife.
He cradles her wrinkled hand in his,

24

stethoscope dangling from his neck,

it had murmured unpleasant things
    —the gossip of blood—
to his ears moments earlier.

Her eyes, clear, sparkle hope. She begs
for him. His eyes try to lie with smiles.
He wonders if he was really her best choice.

Ponders why it is so much easier to lift
a net of nerves from a sea of tissue
or rebuild an intricate lattice work

of arteries and veins in hapless organs
than it is to mend old broken hearts.
The suturing with words, no easier.

He gently lifts her hands into his,
squeezes them ever so softly.
Her bright blue eyes fade

gray, but only for a moment. Her baby
smooth smiles return. She can feel
the pulse of his heart infuse with hers.

Orange Peels

Mom dried the peels of orange; they twisted hard in city air.
Draped them over coals; citrus smoke engulfed us. A sweet
spike for appetites. Defrayed yellow jacket sting-runs. A nuptial
for lemon'd chicken: dripped olive oil, garlic & parsley licked air.

Dad stashed the wine in a grape juice jug under the picnic table.
I was easily bribed to keep quiet with bottom-of-glass sips
in case the beach patrols came with sour looks. Dad winked
at Mom. Her potato salad, with celery seeds, a winner. We'd
steal a bite or two. Winked back. Swore we wouldn't gamble
like that again.

Smell of Chesapeake Bay mingled with damp sand and pine
wood floors. One-arm bandits lined pavilion walls—a juke
box in the corner. The music—whirring clacks of plastic,
the shower of coins as lemons, cherries, and oranges
rastered in the payoff windows.

I lurked in the edges. Too young to play, too broke to sneak
a crank of the handle. Sometimes I'd find an old Buffalo nickel
wedged between the slats of wood streaked with orange clay,
worn down from the shuffle of would-be winners scraping by
floors, their pockets empty; eyes still glazing a pair of sour fruits.

The iPod

Herman stepped gingerly onto the bus—
a forty-five year old man, backpack
low slung cinching the tweed overcoat
that overhung his unclasped galoshes.
He fingered the cleft of his oval plastic
coin purse for quarters and dimes.
Inspected each face for blemishes before
dropping the shiny coins in the slotted
glass box for passage. Shuffled his way

to the back of the bus, past the taunts
and sneers, derision, the unmuffled
laughter. He'd hear, "Here comes
the retard." But Herman looked straight
down at his feet scraping the corrugated
rubber running the length of the bus.
He tripped over one of the hoodlum's
legs stuck out as he neared, and tumbled,
arms spread as if flailing wings for a brief
uncontrolled flight. He crashed into arms
of another ne'er-do-well perched at the end
of the rubber runway—the iPod took-off
from his hands, flew into an aluminum pole
deflecting hard into metal rails, breaking-up
into inoperative hunks of lifeless electronics.

"Sorry, sorry" he said, picking himself up.
The angry punk grabbed Herman by the

collar of his coat and shook him spitting
epithets. An older guy in shirt & tie,
horn-rimmed glasses, absorbed in a Wall
Street journal, stood up
for Herman, exchanged his Clark Kent
demeanor for a couple of steel fists
to the jaws of harassing thugs;
martialled his legs to their chests.

Meanwhile, in a quieter corner
of the flat-gray bus, Herman tinkered
with the broken pieces,
laid them on the dark green cushion
in the back of the bus. His backpack, full
of what-nots and thingamajigs, crazy glue,
wire on a spool, batteries, tweezers
and a Swiss-made pocketknife with mini
screwdrivers and a rasping awl. His tools,
he deftly wielded despite the rumblings
from diesel engine coming through the seat.

He dismantled the iPod cover
hiding the dead circuits; resurrected them
with ingeniousness—a spot welding device:
battery and shorted wires to solder
the wire paths broken in the fall.

When he finished, he polished
the bandaged iPod with his shirt.
The screen brightened with a song
list again and the music played
through the earphones.

The bus driver had called the police;
they came with their billy clubs
in about ten minutes, but the older guy
didn't need any of their help. The punks
complained of Herman's intentional
destruction of the iPod. But the faint
sound of a Rolling Stones' song
spilled out through the earphone
as Herman handed the good-as-new
iPod to the officer... without looking
into his eyes; and the words of
Mr. Jimmy and Mick Jagger chimed out—
something about not always getting
what you want, but if you try
you might get what you need.

They hauled the hoodlums off to jail.
Herman neatly tucked his tools away.
When he came home, his eyes narrowed,
and he said, "Pop, I need a gun,
a soldering gun."

Corn Silk and Violets

Black dirt feels moist through my fingers.
Rich, pungent earth, where the once living
have been distilled into ash and crumbled
leaves, is now a repository for kernels of corn,

pink, as if its lifeblood came from the bones
of the ground. The seeds fold into its bosom,
water sifts through pores, and the green shoots
sprout through earth grasping the sky.

They give back a hundred-fold—each silk ear
tuned to the heartbeat of the universe,
yet each kernel must die first. I wonder
if my daughter knows that.

I peek through the underside of my broad straw hat
through its tightly weaved netting. The kitchen pane,
in partial glare, in partial shadow, obscures her.

But I see her watching me. My eyes glisten
emptiness. Can she feel my silent dreams?

~~~

I creak open the old faucet, mix hot water with the cold,
adjust the temperature just right. A daily ritual,
as if baptism with holy water to sprinkle the fragile

flowers on the sill. Clay pots edged
to catch the sun-mottled shade, now waning.
Forget-me-nots and saintpaulines cling to dirt

as if there's no tomorrow. I wonder if Mom knows
that I love her. I watch her toil through the window
in my kitchen, lost in her own world. All those years, lost.

The violets are especially vibrant today.
Just the right amount of water, the right amount of sun.
Just the right touch of heart.

Mulberry Leaves

An autumn view outside
a nursing home

As if an aftermath of calamity,

               the leaves lay

their hearts splayed on weathered planks
of Douglas fir. The wood striated—a vestige
of arteries. Hardened

        grains pressed flat; pulp, long gone.

Aged pine, a fitting mausoleum for the fallen
leaves withered on their arched backs, twisted.

               Morning light

casts amber against the graying wood; shadows
of sandpaper leaves, smoothed. Their own
medicinal miracles, useless.

           Sweet fruit, gone; wine, too,

               some vinegar

the ground.   Only indigo stains remain.

Roses for a Thornbird

The hard ground gives way to the shovel,
    his boot guiding blade as it knifes the dirt
        for the loaming. Roses—long since withered

on stems with thorns—still grasp, tear
    earth when tossed into the shallow grave
        of a rusted wheelbarrow; stones

clinking bleak metal walls. Without words
    he wheels it to the other part of the garden,
        dumps it in the shadow

of the barnwood shed, still standing after all
    those winters. The starlings complain,
        but a thornbird sings his final song.

Diamonds

      I want to forget.
When I press my eyes closed
to shut out the light, I see
a diamond mine as if the coal
blackness is squeezed until
sparkles grow from the dark.
They turn raven black to purple,
then fly into thick webs of indigo.
In patterns, dots stream
      from inside me,
red, green, transforming to rings
as if pebbles rippling a pool of dark.
      I rub my eyes
through thin fleshy lids. And rings
couple to form trains of yellow
that traffic on invisible rails. Hauling.
They carry me atom-by-atom
in carloads: my carbon, my soul.
      I open my eyes
and it's raining outside. The coal tar
shines in lamplight, the moon
swallowed by clouds.
      I don't see
the hard coal anymore. Disappeared
as dust washed down the black street.
      I blink and it is gone.
      But I want to remember.

The Devil's Head Games

The first time I prayed
for the demons to leave
I could not hear them say no.
The throb in my brain—six dB
above the timpani of pain—
masked their voices.

There was a sulfurous hint
in the air above the Arco Desert.
My bones, dry at this high altitude.
The games that devils play.
They awakened my genes. I never knew
about the headaches hiding there.

Sunlight clamored in my head
with hammers. Morning birds'
whispers bludgeoned my eyes.
And night was no friend.
Even touch of blankets to my face
rasped my brain.

O, if only sleep would come.
Let it bring something more than
useless aspirin-laced codeine, like
empty dreams or hemlock.

Perhaps lobotomy of pain.
Perhaps the sweet stillness of death.

Yet I know
      that joy comes
            in the mourning.

Before the Depression

She reposes on her paisley sofa, a pillow comforting the small of her back; vein-filled hands, patient, poised on the armchair. Hazel-blue eyes—opaque to light, gaze through the window—glisten. She smiles and, as if in a movie theater, sees/hears the child of her childhood sing back in the film, through the black-and-white flickers.

Genesis of Fear (two excerpts)

1954

Who gives a shit what a six-year old feels inside while they're yanking his teeth?

The stove in the doctor's office—enamel white, whiter than his coat—sat against the wall. It seemed to guard the escape door. The glass, pebbled, blocked my view to the outside. The stove's blue flames licked a dark-colored bottle. They dripped the hot chloroform on a cotton bib draped over my face—soon, only darkness. Though I could hear the murmur of voices (Dad's, too), aloneness entrenched its fear in me; felt it stalk me in the darkness with sharp metal tools I wasn't supposed to see: the needles and awls, the gripping pliers. I screamed but no one heard me, except for my monster hiding like a giant cockroach, braced in his corner ready to lunge. How can I escape when there is nothing to see, or any ground beneath my feet? I couldn't run or even move, yet I sensed motion as if tethered to a long, invisible swing. I knew the amusement ride feeling—the tightness of the g's at the bottom of the fast swoop, the light-headed stomach at the top of the downswing. I yelled again and I knew they could hear me: *Stop! I want to get off!* They lied when they said, "Just another moment." They were in my mouth and I could scream no more, but I screamed inside, in the genesis of my fear, in the nauseous darkness that had the sick-sweet smell of death.

2009

The devil must have planned the evolution of fear real well. There's a monster inside of me and I can't even form the form the letters that spell its name. He'll see me and make me cringe—my insides fold to keep the fear trapped. I can't breathe in; only exhale those words on paper. They're blurred now, the parchment soaked with fear. Ink dissolves as if my blood smears the page. Those swaths of words are rational, even funny sometimes, until the next shuddering of my guts and the uncontrolled suppression of my thoughts drip as mucous from my nose. What is this fear that I dare not even think of? It takes so many forms! It is always cocooned inside my mind. Then there's a metamorphosis of a momentary smile into protracted fear; the thing flutters in between breaths. I am asphyxiated with terror. Yes, the thought of needles prick me to the heart and the roaches make me throw up in my mind until my throat is squeezed and my eyes bulge. The thought of loneliness haunts me, hunts me. It prowls into every sanctum I can find until it catches me naked against the wall and swallows me whole before my heart can stop beating. I yell out, but no one can hear me scream inside my mind. I can't even hasten the dying, for that would fulfill the fear of lonely death.

Yet I am horrified that it is killing me even when I'm not looking.

Euroclydon

*After Saint Paul's fourth missionary journey
on an Alexandrian ship (Acts 27)*

When Bora winds did funnel
Through mountain shields of stone
Poised high above the blue turned gray
The ocean churned below

It stole the winter haven
And blew the seething foam
Astern with salty vengeance
That drove them far from home

Towards sifting sands of Sirtis
O'er shattered wooden ribs
This haunted graveyard beckoned
The squalled ill-fated ship

Walls of restless water
Around the vessel poured
Between the swells that foundered
And waves that crashed the floor

Battered rails and gunnels
Yardsail tackle ditched
Along with tons of cargo grain
The ocean swallowed quick

Twisted claws of blackened clouds
Scratched the rain-drenched planks
Grasped to shred men's hope
in which the talons sank

Lightning-fire crackled
Dragon's cyclone breath
Blew and bashed the bow of ship
Drowned the cries of death

For days adrift in endless dark
No guidance from the stars
But Homer's ancient current drove
That hulk of broken spars

Between the prayers and hunger fast
The pounding shore was heard
Paul's dream was surely real for all
And hope again restored

Fifteen fathoms rising fast
Four anchors dragging clay
While eastern wind did thread the ship
To bars of sand that day

Timber torn among the rocks
But not a life was dashed
And some began to know their God
The day the ship had crashed

Author's Notes:

(i) *Euroclydon* is Greek for a nor'easter hurricane-like gale in the Mediterranean Sea.

(ii) *Bora winds* flow from the north over the 8000-ft mountains on the island of Crete.

(iii) *Sirtis* is a treacherous area north of Africa, where many ships have foundered.

(iv) "Homer's current" is what I call the thermohaline current, flowing clockwise in the fall/winter (and counterclockwise in the spring/summer). From the island of Malta (south of Sicily), it proceeds northeast to Greece, then southwest to western Crete before turning westerly toward Malta. It is the same island that Odysseus (the mythical character in *The Odyssey*) and Paul (the Apostle) had shipwrecked on.

Death Approaches

My harp is also turned to mourning
—Job 30:31

It always comes when it's dark. I feel it lurk
trying to get a foothold in the crack of my skin,
in the thinning shadow where I hide. The terror
is soon upon me, my soul is poured out. Death

approaches with a shear garment to bury me.
It drifts in with a foul wind—disease grips
me around the neck, strangles me until I shake
with dust and ashes. And I cry out, yet no one

hears me. The beast lurches, its long-needle
talons pierce my bones, grapple my insides.
My skin turns black with blood, my bones burn.
But in a twinkling of the dawn, its trammel-veil

will tear, its hooks will break to dullness, melt
as if its own dragon's breath was turned upon it.
I will dress in glory of the stars and rejoice.

O death, where is thy sting?
O grave, where is thy victory?
—1 Corinthians 15: 55

Alternative Medicine

I.

Julie's hazel blue eyes glisten in the stark
recesses of her hairless head, not even stubble
from her once flowing auburn locks remain
after chemotherapy.

The half-light in her hospital room illumines
her gaunt face. A thin black-and-white checkered
gown rises and falls with her breathing

that labors in syncopation with the heart
monitor and pulse oximeter—her body starving
for oxygen. Her catheter snakes from under
the sheet to a bedpan full of pale yellow liquid.

And the IV silently drips some miracle chemical,
but now its magic virtually gone. She doesn't worry
anymore about a staph infection where the needle
pierced her vein. Why would she?

The room is antiseptic. That's what the nurses
tell her at every visit, after each surgery, after
all the radiation treatments failed.

No more procedures scheduled. Tomorrow
she goes home, her body ruined, *but healing
is just as important as curing.*

II.

Her husband, Bill, makes her comfortable,
but she doesn't want to hear him say the word
hospice, especially when she's lucid like now.

She rests in her favorite chair—a French provincial—
by the Tiffany lamp; Bill sleeps in the bed
next to her.

The moon is pallid, its light bleeding through
the slats of the window blinds. The Man-in-the-moon
doesn't offer any smiles.

Julie squeezes a stuffed animal
she had since a child—a brown monkey—
close to her chest. Then shakes
it with unexpected violence; curses it
when it doesn't tell her why.

She reaches for the scissors,
and the needle in the nightstand drawer,
but doesn't fill it with insulin. Just air.

The midnight moon is almost blue, and her face
is a ghost. She stares through the seams of night;
doesn't see any stars. Julie clenches the needle.

III.

Bill stirs in the morning light; feels the cold
empty space next to him. Julie's chair

is now turned toward the window. He cries
out to her, but she doesn't answer.

His heart races louder than sunlight
as he jumps out of bed and scrambles to her.
Her face is still pale, the scissors lay open
on the floor,

and the needle, stuck through the heart
of the stuffed animal. Her fingers, ever so
gently, caressing the sheared head

of the brown monkey as if death itself,
as if by just imagining the softness of its skin,
its panting rush into her lap,
that she might tame it.

Quotations adapted from "Hospital Writing Workshop" by
Rafael Campo, MD. See Poem-a-Day, January 3, 2014.

Hospice

I closed my eyes. A warm blue light filled them, and I didn't hurt inside anymore. I breathed the flower-spiced air laced with that sweet song grandma used to sing all the time. In fact, it sounded just like her; seemed to come from a silhouette with outstretched arms. I started walking through a cottony-soft tunnel when I heard your voice, mother, calling me back. I stopped and turned toward the whimpers; strained to open my eyes. It was you singing that song; your lips lilting furtive prayers.

I whispered, *Mother*, your eyes drank my words. After I die, let them have my body to study, I don't want any other kid to be cursed with what I have. Let them take it out, then burn what's left of me. Throw my ashes where you scattered grandma's—in the deep blue lake, in the mountains, with the sun shining on it.

Lilies & Morning Matins

Every sun-filled dawn
        I will steal its colors
                and celebrate until

my throat is crimsoned
        with joy. I will trumpet
                voluntarily your name

to the whole world
        and feel the valley
                fill with fresh light

Your green fields
        washing the sorrow.

Light Blooms

I flash through the dark space
on a moonbeam. On a photon
like the one Einstein talked about
in physics class. Where time
      stands still at this speed,

where mind and heart intersect
with feelings; fact and faith
      emerge from chiaroscuro.

No longer am I a child
of the dark. I have grown
into light and I now can see,
count each glimmer,
      touch each hope—

millions of beams
pierce the darkness,
each one lifting prayers
into the infinities
      as scents of flowers rising.

And I hear the stars sing
as angels. I am not alone
      anymore.

About the Author

John C. Mannone has work appearing in *Windhover, Artemis, 2016 Texas Poetry* Calendar, The *Southern Poetry Anthology* (Volume VII, NC), *Still: The Journal, Pine Mountain Sand & Gravel, Negative Capability, Split Rock Review, Agave, Tupelo Press, Raven Chronicles, Poetica Magazine, Synaesthesia, 3Elements Review, The Baltimore Review, Rose Red Review, Pirene's Fountain, Tipton Poetry Journal, Prairie Wolf Press Review, The Pedestal, Wordgathering, Motif* v2 & v3 anthologies, and others. He has a dark literary poetry collection, *Apocalypse* (Alban Lake Publishing). He won the 2015 Joy Margrave Award for creative nonfiction. He's the poetry editor for *Silver Blade* and *Abyss & Apex,* and an adjunct professor of chemistry and physics in east TN. His work has been nominated three times for the Pushcart Prize. Visit *The Art of Poetry*: http://jcmannone.wordpress.com

www.ingramcontent.com/pod-product-compliance
Lightning Source LLC
Chambersburg PA
CBHW060236180626
46813CB00007B/3111

* 9 780993 049385 *